Lyrically Spoken

Words from the Heart

"An intimate Memoir of Poetry"

By

Melody Toomer

Lyrically Spoken

All rights reserved. No part of this book shall be reproduced, stored in a retrieval system, or transmitted by any means-electronic, mechanical, photocopying, recording, or otherwise without the permission from the publisher. No patent liability is assumed with respect to the use of the information contained herein. Although every precaution has been taken in preparation of this book, the publisher and author assume no responsibility for errors or omissions. Neither is any liability assumed for damages resulting from the use of the information contained herein.

ISBN-10: **0615971131X**
ISBN-13: **978-0615971131**

Library of Congress Control Number: **202912510**

Printed in the United States of America
Author: Melody Toomer
Cover Design/Graphics by Eric's Designs.
Editor-in-Chief: Montice L. Harmon
Associated Editor: Latoya Williams
Interior Designer: Montice L. Harmon
Photography: Joshua Limens

Copyrighted © 2014 by Melody Toomer for BlackBerryPublishing
　　　　All rights reserved

The events in this book are not fictitious. Any similarity to real persons, living or dead is coincidental and not intended by the author.

Published by BlackBerryPublishing©2014
　　　　Atlanta, GA
Printed in the United States of America

Marketed and Distributed by BossWriterPublishing, LLC ©2014

Words from the Heart

Melody Toomer

Acknowledgements

First, I would like to give honor to God for seeing me through this journey. I also would like to thank my grandmother, Orsie P. Harris for her positive words throughout my life as a child to an adult.

I would like to thank everyone that supporting me, by buying this book. I pray this brings understanding and peace to all the lives that read it. I would like to give a special shout out to all the people who said I could not make it, or would not see the day this book was published. Your words encouraged me to keep pushing through past my obstacles.

Thank-You!

Sincerely,
Melody Toomer

Lyrically Spoken

Editor Reviews

Without a doubt this book was destine to be a part of this world. Every poem filled my heart with sympathy for Melody's trials and tribulations.

~ Latoya Williams

After reading this book, my life changed forever. I was lost, now I am found. I can only imagine going through what this poet experienced in life. I found this book to be well told, formatted and delivered with strength.

~Patrick Thomas

Rave Reviews

The way this story told and formatted changes the way memoirs are written.
~ James Henderson

Melody Toomer's life reflection is needed in the black community. Her story relates.
~ Joyce Remy

Words from the Heart

Melody Toomer

Lyrically Spoken

Taken

I am staying faithful to my spouse; do not come around here running your mouth. You are trying to mess up a happy home but my single days are all gone. Therefore, you can say what you want to.

Keep feeding my head with lies. I know the truth as we hold each other at night. You can offer me all the money in the world and material things. However, here is where I am staying why I would leave something so good.

That lasts for a quick wine and dine I want a lifetime. You want me to have a couple drinks with you, and then before you know it you are asking can I spend the night. Please understand I have heard those lines before, but it does not motivate me to knock on your door.

You are asking for a quick fix, you can throw around your money it does not impress me. What does is someone who loves every ounce of me. "Just stop while you're ahead." I cannot see what lead you to speak, you were doing you and I was doing me

"*Just face it… I'm taken.*"

Words from the Heart

Melody Toomer

Evil Letting Go

You always portray cruelty; questioning my intentions; Act as if you are angry from the sight of my existence. You provoke me to control my actions get furious when my soul is relaxing.

You just cannot perceive the happiness deep inside of me. It confuses you and consumes you, interrogating your soul. Because of the bitterness, you cannot yet let go.

You drive off pain; you must be insane, because the life you are draining out of people is nothing worth gaining. It shows your ignorance and arrogant character that you do not see.

Why must you hate me because god's light dwells in me? At first, you drove me to depression. However, as time went on learning that it is just a Lifelong lesson.

That teaches me not to let anything, but the almighty abide in me. I want let you take my soul, my actions I will control, god's grace will unfold, and for you spirit of deception I am letting you go.

Lyrically Spoken

Complete

You have filled that missing piece; with a love so concrete; specializing in only my feelings and me. Demonstrating my emotional healing;
So innocent and pure, negativity does not exist I do not have to endure.

The pain and the hurt that usually comes naturally "notice its absence?"
What we have flow's like the waves on the ocean shore.
Since birth, we were connected to the core.

My purpose was the completion of my destiny; it was finished.
The exact moment you looked at me. I knew then I had found the answer to my existence, the gift for my persistence.

I found in you and what god has created no man can undo.
You are the example of what this world has been longing for.
Then surprisingly you knocked on my door.
What a relief in this season, a blessing in this meeting.
Now I realized the reason for my prayers.

In addition, the confidence I displayed that you were always out there. With a reflection of me in your soul, a feeling I never let go. I knew we would finally meet now destiny is complete.

Words from the Heart

Melody Toomer

Deeply Sympathetic

The ones without shelter are food sleeping on the cold streets. That begged for something to eat as their beaten until they bleed. They have no family to run too. No more friends to help them make it through their appearance are dirty dehydrated and thirsty not feeling worthy. Turning to drugs for comfort because they feel too lone some just want to be free with no privacy in their conditions no growth are friendly visits. They have experienced the true meaning of poverty without the luxury of currency. I sympathize compassionately they have settled in their situation.

Which further complicates their days and controlling their ways suffering among their race. Sleeping under bridges but what you consider inhumane, they just consider it living. With a victim mentality, this is definitely reality, the things that society try to forget the things we do not have time to deal with.

Lyrically Spoken

Snake of mine

I loved you and cared for you dearly did anything I could. To see you happy no matter if I went lacking. But it's sad to say that none of that matters. You played your position until an opportunity occurred. You thrive off seeing me hurt. You drug my name in the dirt. As if you never really loved me, it is tragedy the pain you inflict; no time ever could imagine I would be your next victim. So you can destroy me slowly with your venom deserve so much better than loose. From someone I trusted you are corrupted I will never understand you plan to drag me down.

Until my happiness no longer found camouflaged with this depression could you be my lesson. learn from this as your venom runs through my blood stream!

Was thus foreseen yet my loving being blinded me of the unthinkable. My life is valuable yet you are trying to take my breath. Is this my test I must confess as the life drains out of me? That this snake all along was my enemy. However, my blinded eyes did not find the time.

To let lose this snake of mine…

Words from the Heart

Melody Toomer

Sick

My heart is flustering with a pain, Head is hurting with a migraine Tossing and turning cannot sleep. Stomach growling but I cannot eat. Just spend my time listening to love songs.

Replaying the day, you left me, how did it go wrong? I am constantly checking my phone to see if I have a missed call. I cannot stop staring at your picture on the wall.

I am going through withdrawal missing what we had I am so depressed it feels like my heart will fall out my chest. Sweating, regretting how I hurt you. I did not know until now how much I love you. I have been awakening by reality and now I am sick.

Lyrically Spoken

Free Myself

Chains will be broken I see when your approaching and I walk away. It's hard to befriend a person who constantly hate. Then there motives are for your destruction.

You're standing by watching, waiting, and wishing for my downfall. Keep praying for my failure discouraging me from success. Because you do not understand and haven't figured out your calling yet.

Therefore, you influenced me to be just as foolish as you are in the street. By making ignorant decisions, getting locked up accepting defeat. However, I will never be your puppet for display.

I have a mind of my own and it does not indulge to your negative ways. I will continue to surround myself with a person that has profound intellect not someone who can't see past this hood mess.

Words from the Heart

Melody Toomer

Today's Pain

At this moment, and time, experiencing turmoil in my life, I want this day to end because I am weakened by it so tired of crying and stressing. Thinking positive seems so hard to do when the world is on top of you.

My expectations are little to none, and I do not understand where it all came problem after problem I have no idea how to solve them. Giving up is not an option. My mind already has reached its limit of being cluttered.

If it's not one thing it's another it's so hard to stay sober I can't wait until this day is over. I'm confident that tomorrow will be better than today eventually this pain will go away.

Then produce a brighter day at least that's what I'm convincing myself to allow my mind relief. But it's nothing concrete as of today I'm emotionally trampled by my fears but tomorrow hasn't even got here.

I'm losing it all, going insane, because of my insecurities of what remains is today's pain.

Lyrically Spoken

Virginity

It is the most precious gift in this world and that is exactly the reason why Immediate attention. Your temple is equal to the green grass in the summertime. It is a treasure of uniqueness that is not meant for everyone just that special someone. Be careful and not naive bearings of the fight from the other species.

He is fighting for credibility among their peer. Whispering special thing's in your ear. They stimulate your mind with a motive within their heart. With dishonest intentions, you remain "cautious" your emotions are tangled in a web of lies.

Never summit unless he makes you his wife. Stand firm in your belief then you will finally see. The lengths some men will go just for your virginity. To get recognized by their friends for being the one who broke you in then you're left with nothing but a reputation that you are promiscuous even though he is your first that doesn't guarantee that's what he'll converse.

Your worth waiting for no matter what is said do not do something you will soon regret.

Words from the Heart

Melody Toomer

Why?

It is as if I am talking to a brick wall trying to push out some remorse. You are grown and should not have to be forced. You are supposed to treat others with respect and love .Especially when their providing when they are not obligated. My kindness was exaggerated. Really is that your truth I believe you are so foolish.

How can you take from your blood? Why treat them, as they are just another person in this world? I let you into my comfort zone now I see its less stressful being alone. I cannot believe the betrayal you supplied. However, for once in my life you will be rejected. I will not allow you to control my day-to-day moods.

Peace is the only emotions I choose so if I have to let you go it was because you were for a season. I'm above your harsh words and cruel actions that's exactly the reason why I'm leaving.

Behind This Smile

Behind this smile is a little girl trapped with suppressed feelings. Tormented by pain barely dealing with what this world considers living. Feeling emptiness in my innocence wish, I could stop these tears from entering my Adulthood I had to find my own way on this narrow road reaching out for god as the devil approach. Telling me I was not needed anymore follow me just let go. Disgracing me with worldly thing has to cover up all my spiritual pain.

However, inside its broken piece's to this puzzle it is so dark in this tunnel. Where is the light to perfection? What about all the money I invested for a greater cause now I'm emotionally smothered by these four walls I'm isolated with time to think a miracle's coming so I'm scared to blink.

Finding a love on earth a love that revealed this little girl's hurt. I had to pull away and continue this image of a brighter day. Therefore, I heard the word's that reached me from heaven telling me what god expected. Therefore, I follow his footsteps in the sand and realized He is all that I really needed in a man so I stick by his side for a WHILE. AS GOD heals THIS WOMAN behind this smile.

Melody Toomer

Bringing Me Down

I have realized and noticed your deception. Secretly working against me not knowing I am catching it all. Every attempt you make against my failure. Because you acknowledge my being is special.

Therefore, my prayers reach out to you with hopes that it inspires you to change. Obviously, some insecurity triggers your rage. I am going to stay humble despite what you do.

Your jealousy is shining through you. Past your hating spirit, I will hold my head to the light. Your negativity is not allowed to make me cry. I will not give you my energy.

Even though you fend for ownership, I will not give you an ounce of it.

Complicated

Sun setting and your still not home once again I am home alone. You keep ignoring my phone calls making me feel so small. Then when you finally dark through the door walking around and I am completely ignored. Cannot communicate you claim you need your space. I wish this pain would disappear when you catch ghost. I continue pacing the floor no one to wipe my tears.

I deserve so much better than this negative presence. All this wasted time I invested. We have chemistry no longer a connection tired of all this shortly affection. Makes me sick to my stomach my heart and intuition tells me it is another woman. However, I have no proof I am so confused but I can smell her pheromone all over you.

Honestly you are a coward and you constantly stress me out I would not feel our love disappear if we were never involved. Sexually frustrated but yet you want look my way. I even cried as you turned me down wearing my sexiest lingerie this is getting pathetic. I cannot drift away from the truth the reality is your no longer attracted and our relationship is through. I cannot make you love me love me anymore. I am going to let you be free because our relationship has run its course.

Melody Toomer

Killing me

I see you with her passing by wearing a smile. Jealousy takes over my flesh I wish I was not your ex. I was never ready for it to end but it did. Now I have to face the fact that you have moved on. However, I have been single still holding on. Hoping one day you would return.

Everything in me yearns for what we had. It is as if my fairytale turned out bad. As fast as a blink of an eye, damn I want you back in my life. However, you seem happy from that wide dazzling smile. You both seem compatible. I loved you enough to let you leave. Now this emptiness is killing me.

Soon

I am waiting on your lesson, no need for second-guessing. The tables will change give it a second. Then you feel the pain you have inflicted towards my pain. Only then, you will think about your past transgressions.

It is destined to become your reality partly because you never valued me you took my heart for granted. The cycle will repeat in your season. Bless your heart for the tragedy you will be seeing.

It is a part of life and the learning process. One day we all will break hearts. It will become a chapter you soon will regret. Your mistakes you will quickly confess. Some call the circle of life others call it fate.

Melody Toomer

Frequently

You run across my mind throughout the day. As if, I cannot retain my thoughts. Could this be feelings I caught? Is this the reason you follow me to my dreams?

I just cannot believe this hold you have on me. This feeling is so sweet. Make's me have faith in true love's intentions so glad that I have witnessed.

The beginning stages to something spectacular. Could I be falling in love with your character? I do not comprehend I cannot even pretend. That the way I feel not guaranteed because you dwell in my heart frequently.

Lyrically Spoken

Next Life

All of humanity has to one-day leave earth! One day our soul will have to disperse. This fact was acknowledged since birth. Our friends and love ones must be left behind. This is just the way god designed it to be. He gave us a choice to choose our future for eternity. He promised to forgive any impurity as long as we repent.

It cannot be prevented so we might as well live everyday like it's our last. Every individual must experience what it feels like to pass. Go to another place and prepare for judgment day. We all will meet Christ so prepare for your next life.

Words from the Heart

Purpose

I have worked without recognition slaving for something different. Focused on my responsibility, settling with the majority, living in doubt, and drowning in my regret's. Without fulfillment, I have fallen victim to statistics just existing confused and in pain. Yet my purpose remains in my heart. Naive about where to start, so I dream of something greater than I do, which is my destiny.

I tried to put on hold however, my testimony must be told to help someone along the way. I have a story to tell before I reach the grave. My mind want rest anticipating the day this burden will be lifted off my chest. Then the angel will sing in my behalf and I will not be defeated. Because my work on earth will be completed.

Lyrically Spoken

Speaker

I'm going to share my life with the world so all the little boys and girls can find comfort in there situation's I want to encourage the little ones to never give up and to pray to ask God for guidance in this cruel world. I will be ecstatic to tell the world my testimony in hopes that it would change the perception of their minds instead of being confined with a buildup of pain, emptiness, and abandonment. I just want to be that one to make everyone love and forgive sometimes it is hard to swallow that pill but I'll be there support system that way all of the

"Sickness in this life will be eliminated"

Words from the Heart

Melody Toomer

Father

I wish that I knew you and you knew me. I think about you constantly and how you abandoned your child, your content with your decisions. Just to think you did not see me take my first step, never wiped my eyes as I wept. No visits to the school, sometimes I looked for you. Yet, you were nowhere to be found. I prayed for your safety even though you were not around. I prayed that one day I would see your face, and you say baby everything is going to be okay. God took my mother home, yet, you are not gone. We live in the same state, but as I pass, you quickly look away. Then I think to myself, I am your child without the holidays and birthdays, you telling me you love me before you walk away. You are so coldhearted. I still remember the day we departed. I spoke my mind in a sickening voice as I cried so much. My voice became hoarse that day you looked me in my eyes and said you are no longer my child. How is it possible you can make this decision? You did not make it when you and mom had relations. Therefore, why let me go now and kick me out in the rain. Your child that shares your last name, the blood that ruins through my veins is the same as yours. I have been biologically your responsibility but your were never available you want to forget I exist yet I kept trying with much persistence to fix our relationship but as you said you was not having it.

Innocence stripped

Lying here on a platform of misery inhaling cheap cologne, sweat dripping on my physique likes my tears grieving in need of assistance. Yet, no one hears my voice grunting noises drown out my voice as you abstract my innocence for your satisfaction, forcing your way into my soul, while my lifeless frame lies there stiffen with confusion in my eyes. How can you ignore my loud cries I resisted until I was converted to weak as I screamed until my voice screeched you've exhausted me with this forcible violation is all my mind conceive as I lie here half naked self-esteem demolished, as I ask God why me trying to cease this pain as IMP slapped to the side. What possess you to glorify my destruction, ache my wound, as it ruptures as you finally come to an halt. I lie there silent, as you walk away with your plan only to ejaculate inside of me. There is a seed that grows from my defiled situation now I am carrying a baby inside of mer. What do I do? God helped me through the weather abortion or adoption this is a day, that will never be forgotten.

Melody Toomer

Believe

Think beyond what you see you have the power to be what you want to be you have to use your imagination in order to succeed where am I going to be years from now imagine greatness Then things that will make you proud only then will your imagination turn to reality but not without performing to the best of your ability anything in life you can achieve but you can't be insecure you must believe everyone possess a calling were all here for a purpose don't let life pass you by feeling hopeless you must take risks and at least try your best and realize the obstacles you're going through is only a test which makes you a stronger person and its preparing you for your purpose so when it feels as if weights are on your chest remember that trouble doesn't last always your testimony was first a test.

Lyrically Spoken

In the name of love

Pain heading straight for my heart evolving until I'm parentally scarred from the stress the pain you cause I was deranged to ever feel you were the one the beginning was filled with laughter and love it was no doubt you had all my trust you took advantage of me loving you hasn't been easy I made a commitment thought everything was peachy but all the infidelities, pain and dishonesty is making me want to take another avenue I can no longer disguise the truth I gave my all too you and only you while you gave me your love and to a selected few I deserve someone who appreciates me as a woman and someone who will fight for my love because I'm not common you'll never find the name of love how I provided everyday of your life you'll be reminded of how you made a mistake what goes around comes back around I guess you can call it fate my plan is to find myself again it's not my job to condemn you for your mistakes and I refuse to get in a rage just want to display my gratitude for this lesson even though there's a lot of unpleasant memories I wouldn't have it any other way one day you're going to stare love in the face and fall so deeply and become needy then be rejected after all the love you've invested then your memories will return to me then you will see just how hurtful the name of love can truly be.

Words from the Heart

Melody Toomer

Feelings

Can't control emotionally trampled by my thoughts. Because you're involved with this all revolves around your significant other. I'm in a love triangle, hoping one day you come to your senses while sitting at home waiting on your call or text. I guess you're better half hasn't left yet. I truly regret being in this situation I wish I could have her out the equation so it can be me and you. My feelings are SEEPING through, and I think I'm in love with you. How did I get to this place?

Let me take a minute to concentrate and eliminate this problem. How did I hit rock bottom when you explained your situation. When we meet that day, why didn't I follow my conscience and walk away. Now it's too late, I'm in too deep and I know you want leave her for me. You have too much integrity to leave your family, but what about me. Do I even matter? Are does having us both what you rather I have to break free. Because this loneliness is taking over me, being the other woman I was willing, damn, these uncontrollable feeling.

Lyrically Spoken

Dedication

Move further along past these stumbling blocks. What good is a leader without his flock plant your feet on this blessed land. Success first starts with a plan. There will be obstacles in which you will face. However, hold your head high and not be ashamed of your vision. Embrace it is your responsibility to be destined for greatness God gave you the gift. You must portray it and touch hearts and save souls.

We were created to be his vessel, do criticize neither you nor others, or except failure. This is just a long road in this chapter the book is not finished let all eyes be witness as you prosper and doors open for you the almighty will see you through he knows your heart and the way you feel he's about to make your dreams finally become real.

Words from the Heart

Melody Toomer

Goes public

Dealing with your abusive spouse for years hurting you, and being the exact reason for your tears. However, I never seen it coming if I did I would have started running. As fast as a blink of an eye the side of my head was ruptured.

My heart was punctured, with a sphere your abusive relationship brought us here. While the blood runs down my face, I look around the crime scene blood scattered on the wall and pouring on my sheets. Feeling so weak, I lie down on the bed I hear conformation but no one is acknowledging my head.

I call god's name softly lord please let them look my way.
Then my prayers were answered the ambulance eventually took me away. The deacon started lying to police next thing you know I was on the headlines of the city newspaper was supposed to be anonymous what a way to be famous.

Nobody understood what was going on because in church we wore a mask of disguise. I think to myself finally it is at the surface all of the dark lies. As everyone is speechless focused on me my full attention is on the newspaper local news and how he or she publicized me.

Lyrically Spoken

This is Me!

I have been called a sinner a backslider but I am a realist I am not ashamed to embrace my difference. I am a lover a friend a lover and a queen that believes in the power of the sky. I cry I get depressed I have no shame in getting on my knees to confess to a higher power. I have been called a coward, ugly, and remedial but it does not defend my character.

I have been told id never is successful and that I am too much in the world for god to help. I have been judged on the regular been lead to believe I was not special. However, through all the rumors and tears god brought me here. A person no one believed could make it a person diagnosed crazy.

Through the entire negative placed on my life. I relied on the power and not man and here I am taking a stand. I am pushing all negative energy out my plans so I can focus on the coming. All your perceptions of me are lesson I am still learning.

This is me…

Words from the Heart

Different

I have had my share of broken hearts and empty promises had my name degraded as if I was not a woman. Cried many nights praying for an angel to sweep me off my feet I searched hi and low then started questioning. The existence of true love until you gave me hope something was appealing and so different.

You covered my wounds with your cares sheltered my soul with promises of always being here. For some odd reason I believed in everything you said your words replays in my head. I am so scared yet I feel safe you love me in such a different way it makes me want to face tomorrow.

You took away all sorrow and fears I had about finding something new. It started the day I first looked at you. You never came with an attitude as you had something to prove. Just a humble spirit that explained I love you yea we have had perfection then rocky days.

However, every time I see your smile all the pain goes away and I forget our confrontation. In a split second were love making I enjoy every moment of this life I am living were compatible through spirit. I am so blessed to have someone so different. A needle in the haystack and I want turn my back ill work hard every day to see that this lasts.

Failure wins Victory

Walking around in a complete circle sometimes, I wish my mistakes reversal. It started with procrastination now my motivation exceeds. However, my journey misleads me every time I try to fall to my feet. I get up and keep moving with this burden buried in my heart.

I try to disregard the negative and focus on what is at hand. However, every time I end up finding a dead end and falling in the sand all over again. Therefore, I continue to pursue all the things that I deserve to have. Speaking positive unto the universe waiting on its arrival. Looking at my situation as if it is a chapter in survival.

I am so close yet so far away so persistent have not even slept in days. I am running off adrenalin my time is coming I can't help but continue it. Eventually I see all my blessing behind the scene reaching the surface. All this hard work is paying off it was definitely worth it. From all of my fails attempting to live out my dreams now I am finally seeing was only a stepping-stone towards my victory.

Melody Toomer

If you do not stand for something...

Working without a purpose treated unfairly is it all worth it. You have a voice to set things right yet you sit there believing this is just your life. This is not the way it has to be if u does not stand for something, you fall for anything. Fight for your rights and the laws of the land let them know you are not ignorant you highly understand. In addition, even though you have held on to this so long you know god will guide your footsteps to move on. Changes needs to be in your life you will not be degraded, behind a price. Where are the morals today? Has it dispersed where the brave people that have not lost their soul to the world. That if believe in something greater and spread their message for all generations.

Lyrically Spoken

Bipolar Diagnosed

with a sickness that man created trying to make my life even more complicated as if being black isn't enough and all because my emotions erupts which is a natural action no one is always relaxing taking pills that's prescribed all because once.

I had thoughts of suicide in my mind. However, my mind remained powerful. When negativity enters your brain it is easy to hear something and believe it pills supposed to make my condition better but it only makes me feel under weather there saying it is an imbalance in my brain. However, they really just want to intensify my pain, making me insane so in court they will have the sickness to blame.

I am controlled by this medicine, now I cannot complete daily activities. Now you'll rather give me disability to take me out the workforce because the pills you prescribed makes me worse makes me feel remedial and hi that man made diagnosis took away my life now I'm dependent and I'm immediately the victim addicted as everyone witnesses this drug take away my spirit the person I was no longer existed.

Words from the Heart

Melody Toomer

Picture

Where I am why am I missing from your photo album?
Was I not captured from the flash?
Am I considered the family outcast?
Am I not photogenic are is my existence not worth mentioning?
Am I being to frank are not frank enough?
Is it my lifestyle you want to cover up?
Are we still kin, am I brushed aside? As if, I am from another dimension.
Will my dark skinned complexion stand out?
Is it the way I live which have you distraught?
Did I disappoint you? If I did, I did not try to.
Do you feel as if you are better than me is it easier to tear down my self-esteem?
In order to build yours is that why you drown me with spiteful words?
Am I failures in your eyes are just failure enough not to be involved with photo time?

Get Away

Sometimes I just want to flee have some privacy and breath just venture off from the struggles. Forget all about my troubles and be distant from the things I dislike. Then appreciate god's creations and my life as I find peace in such a lovely atmosphere.

As I am receiving the gift to think clearly, I just want to disappear from what is normal. No being formal just being myself and acknowledge all the tears I left behind. Finally I am free within my mind not one complaint could I find. As I lie down with a visual of the sky, so I close my eyes with the wind caressing my skin. Then my healing begins taking all that is not pure all things that I had to endure.

Then exchanging it with a lasting joy and an also a powerful feeling of being content. A feeling this real has to be heaven sent. Before I fall asleep I marinate on what stresses I would have endured if I never got away.

Melody Toomer

Cuddle

Let me hold you close while our temperature increases its chilly outside and this is where I would rather be. I want to feel us caressing my intentions is not sex. Just want to relax between the sheets with your body touching me.

I guarantee that you will enjoy this body heat before your eyes get heavy. A masterpiece the way our naked bodies adjoin. Looking for a warm spot, so I reach for your loin the cold is not affecting us two because our body is glued. Cannot fall asleep without explaining I love you. One of the best things of being a couple is when it is cold outside.

Time to cuddle

Be careful

One night of passion can turn to a lifetime of regret. Before intimacy, you had better get them checked. Because lies turn to cries and can quickly ruin your life. Do not matter if they looked at you deeply and said baby I am just fine. Those words cut like knife in the end.

When the result finally come in and reads positive. It is imperative that you follow your instincts. The wrong decision could leave you extinct. Some people work to infect as many people as they can. All because they thrive off sweet revenge. Your pain is their gain even if you are negative. They will work even harder to teach you a lesson of destruction.

At the last minute, you realize they are erupting inside of you. Making this disease run through your bloodstream now you wish you could undue your actions. However, the damage is already happening the disease is attacking your white blood cells. You should have cared about yourself you would not be in this situation. All because you could not control the infatuation which is an opening for other complications.

Melody Toomer

Blessed

If you are alive with life within you walking and talking, it is because the man upstairs is giving you a chance to continue. If you had obstacles coming your way and they all magically disappeared, it is because he interfered. If you can breathe in this season, it is because god needed you for something else.

If you were ill and not feeling yourself he cared brought you back to health because your testimony is not finished yet. When your bills are due he already knew check the mailbox and say thank you. Stressed in need of a healing you had better start kneeling and he's sure to start clearing your path.

However, do not look back god is getting your life back intact ignore the distractions. He is working in your life for your satisfaction. If you are without shelter look towards the sky and he is already helping behind the scenes. Life it is all about believing what you cannot see using your imagination and allowing god to be your navigation.

He never does what you expect a he keeps showing up in your life because you are truly blessed.

Degrading Yourself

Dressing provocative leaving nothing for the imagination, you do not understand what it means to be a woman. However, gets mad when someone calls you out you name could you honestly say there to blame.

Being ignorant, loud and obnoxious walking around almost topless but you, want respect tells me is that what your appearance reflect. Wonder why you are not taken off the market you are an easy target do not have to put in much work to lift up your skirt. Is that the kind of attention you want?

You are a queen and should act the part are not you tired of the sexual remarks? Cannot even have an intellectual conversation because their focus is in the infatuation. Do not hear what you saying as they observe the plumpness of your curves. Face it all concentration is on you running around half-naked.

Melody Toomer

Freedom

A world without boundaries, however, still not free condemning me. I cannot move around from the shackles on my feet. I'm controlled by the ones with higher authority, and it's a tragedy polluting my inner peace. Hear me clearly, as I confess all this mess changing my very mood, were programmed to follow ridiculous laws and rules even took the word out of schools. However, talking about legal murders in the history books, the system is a bunch of crooks with backwards outlooks, making us follow suit-putting regulations on everything we do. Remember the days our ancestors suffered to bruises on their back, which did not last. They are still portraying that maybe no longer physically but inflict us with pain mentally drugs on the streets. Whom you think put it there do not act as if you were not aware dope boys pushing ounces now the new announcing bodies' dead killer fled. It has no possibility of being the feds were not using brain cells. Gun shops crooked cops open your eyes and watch as the system plots for us to kill each other, blackmailing under covers condemning you because you are poor, and had to hustle it. We all will be revealed, notice that all the things doesn't appear as frequently in the suburbs in comparison to when you faced with poverty moving backwards.

Broken

Deal with your demons from the past that is the only way you will last in this cruel world. Because there will be more confusion you will endure and in order to with stand you have to be pure. Of all the old memories, remember you are not the first these things repeated for centuries.

You must practice self-healing that is the only way you can surpass being a victim. Being cluttered with baggage from your past will make things harder in your future.

You must let things go because you are the consumer. Life will pull you down to your lowest point and have you at a standpoint if you do not confront your problems. You must have a clear mind and a clear heart embrace your trial that is a start.

Remember people go through things everyday this is something you will experience until you reach the grave. Hold your head hi do not be ashamed you are on earth for a reason it is not a mistake.

Your testimony is unique you can help others so they want repeat your mistakes but you cannot be easy to break. A broken child becomes a broken adult you are the only one who can change that result.

Melody Toomer

Desperate woman

Being degraded to say you have a man putting up with things like you does not understand. Your worth so you allow him to hurt you constantly then you desperately holds on. Without seeing your worth and just moving on. He verbally, physically and emotionally abuse. Your family tries to intervene but you make up an excuse. You claim you have a love so deep but it never stopped him from going out to creep beating you unconsciously. Is it worth the agony you feel?

Do you love this man more than the gift to live? You cannot be serious must be delirious from all the beatings are not you tired of smothering yourself with makeup before meetings. He has broke your spirit down to low self-esteem caused your heart to internally bleed. Is the thing you speak of love?

Is it just camouflaged by your comfort zone? Could you be prone to this way of life? Are just holding on to a fairy tale of him making you his wife? Do not lower your standards for some man! A man that does not love you enough not to lift up his hand.

Almost There

We have invested so much time and energy to see a lasting relationship. Worked on one accord now it's about fixed we struggled we cried and wanted to give up our ammunition was always our love but we strived for perfection and got really close, and it wouldn't of worked out without putting god first. Preparing for this day was a little stressful but definitely, worth the wait it took some understanding and enormous amounts of faith we had to embrace each other difference and acknowledge who we were.

Then change some things in order for this to work as I stand here ecstatic in my white dress I go down memory lane to see our progress. Tears of joy falls down my face as I gaze in your eyes you smile. It said for better are worse for richer are poor.

I feel so secure in what the minister said because without a title we never fled. In this moment in time, I realize the instinct of your care baby we are almost there.

Melody Toomer

Beautiful

Your facial features are unique so easy to want to keep you all to myself. A Sight to see your existence beauty from another dimension my eyes are captured my emotions is ecstatic. I am intrigued to the point of no return continuously want to be in your presence my body yearns. Yearns in excitement anytime you come my way my words disperse and I can't find the words to say

You are a masterpiece, and I want to be apart this picture. I'll venture off to your destination just to see that beautiful face and that smile I haven't felt this way in a while you seduce me with your eyes humble me with your smile I must admit your beauty makes me submit every time you come around me.

I fend for your presence for eternity. I have never seen anything this eye catching and I do not mind investing every part of my day to see the different expressions you make. It's amazing I can concentrate you make me feel joy when my day isn't going great your picture perfect, knowing you is definitely worth it so wonderful your being is beautiful

Scared Of Commitment

We have been implementing a cycle that is not changing hanging on to something that is not worth hanging unto. I have realized what is true from your infidelities even in our marriage all this time this burden I have carried trying to work it out because of the potential I have seen wanting a fairytale as if I seen on TV. However, this is reality is not the same? Make believe how it can be with you continuously cheating, every time your guard is down and I move closer to your heart, you rebel against it and I am scarred still holding on to the invisible actions of you hoping one day our commitment will sink through. Loving you is so hard with you fighting me when I get close you push me to my feet not literally.

This is just a bad dream, at least, which is what I will try to make myself believe without confronting reality. Such a load I'm carrying, sharing you with others acting as if I don't know about you secret undercover so I hold my head down as you walk by smelling sex knowing our commitment is a lie I can't keep going through this repeat all this cheating I have witness and the excuse you gave was your scared of commitment.

Melody Toomer

Wake Up!

You have been sleeping while the world pass you by you have common sense yet you still rely on the entertainment in this world. Knowing it is just an illusion to hide what is really going on. What if it all was gone then will you find the motivation to think on your own.

Technology has sunk you in to its way of life. We have become the victim relying on what we find in the search engine. It's ridiculous yet fun but it has only just begun eventually life as we know will perish technology exposure will increases our minds will decrease all because were naive.

It will manifest into something mind blowing but were sleeping we have no way of knowing what's going on soon this entertainment we love so much will make the world as we know it so much more corrupt then we'll look back at the beginning of everything and wish we would've seen this world perishing.

Lyrically Spoken

Cupids Mistake

I've been hit with the illusion of love actors pretending it's enough They go on believing ill never figure out their true characters. Distracting me with the laughter, they bring to my life. However, I noticed your double faces and it is not anything nice. Therefore, I played my position as a naïve individual.

Your acts of being manipulating showed you were a professional. I had to get out of cupids reach this was a serious mistake. Built with so much hate you are stuck in your ways. You have been breaking hearts so long it is a natural reaction.

You have been content with this way of life so much you do not have a conscience to think twice. You are a camouflaged distraction now I wish cupids arrow would have kept passing.

Words from the Heart

Melody Toomer

Too Late!

I understand you want to pled your case and give it another try. However, let me be the judge of that leave it to me to decide. Let me equal out the pros and the cons to see if you deserve to be a part of my life again to rejoin my world.

You see I repeatedly gave you chances while my friends called me stupid. You claimed you changed but let your actions prove it. I have had enough of your lies and broken promises.

You say you love me but in that, I have no confidence. The trust has disappeared but never has my tears. You have never paid attention to the cries of my heart now you are begging and pleading for yet another shot. Do not know if I can allow you into my plans you will never understand.

How much I gave to this relationship and with all my hard work you never valued it. Not even respecting how I feel you thought you could hide your affair but through prayer, it was revealed. I guess things did not work out.

Is that why your running back to me? I am not showing any compassion you do not deserve my sympathy. The best thing for you to do is move on because the chances I gave you before it is all gone.

Lyrically Spoken

Unnecessary

You stare at me with disgust as if I do not belong here. I will not adjust to your ways you display ignorantly while you discriminate against me tightening your purse as I pass you on the street.

Proving the negative outlook you have about me. I do bleed red just as you do so why treat me as a barbaric fool. I work hard like you nothing comes easy so why do you feel as if I am beneath thee.

It is unnecessary but I cannot change your mentality you are going to proceed in stereotyping me. This is sad that society cannot let go of the past. We cannot have better days because we have judged based on skin race.

Which is morally wrong but the world is dominantly prone to this way of life. It proves the world is not that bright to repeat the same mistakes that sparked hate in so many Americans. In addition, this cycle is what generations to come inherit.

Words from the Heart

Melody Toomer

Suffer Anymore

I will work extra hard in my lifetime so my kids will not. My motivation is seeing them never to go without. I would rather suffer the pain and hardship of becoming a success. Then to let them live one day being in distress.

I know what it means to go without I felt its raft in my prime. It will cause your mind to become weak in attempting any crime. This is not something that I want my kids to feel.

When my persistence pays off my investments will be their shield. They will know that I loved them beyond measures. When the almighty takes me to heaven and I will be content in knowing their okay.

Because I have worked constantly all the way to the grave, so they would not have too. Then they would be able to pursue life with no restraints. Say I am blessed with no complaints struggle then they will no more without an ounce of remorse.

Lyrically Spoken

Mind of a player

I am sorry I hurt you did not mean to make you cry but I cannot keep living a lie. The commitment you want I cannot give you. I will not be tied down that is just something I cannot do. I am addicted to this nightlife please understand I find satisfaction in a one nightstand. I am not making plans to settle down and as hard as it seems I still want you around.

I will not change so do not try to make me I know right now you think I am crazy. However, honesty is key I know I should have told you from the beginning. Therefore, that is my fault but we can still hangout because as of now I do not want to just walk out. I know it is going to take some time to process my request I hope you agree because I am not finished with you yet.

I want to chill one day out of the week that day would be designed especially for you and me. Do not call any other days cause I want be free well I guess it is time to leave please give my cell a ring.

Words from the Heart

Melody Toomer

Almost Took My Life

The impact of seeing your speeding car come my way. I promise I saw my body in a grave. I felt this was the end of my days. How could someone display this much hate? Sure, I wanted to retaliate but god did not see fit. I looked in your eyes after the second hit. I knew the evil forces possessed you to do it. Are words enough these days to make you want to lose it? Then try to take a life that was never yours. Yet I had sympathy for your possessed situation. If I didn't I would of left the state to take all four babies. I could have pressed charges but the kids played in my mind. As they stood at the door watching their mom try to take auntie's life. They cried in terror, as you never gave up your possessed spirit never showed one ounce of love. I could have come back. I knew where you lived, but as I lied crying at night, God changed how I feel now. I walk around in healthy condition I am so thankful to be still living. I figured God would handle you better than I could. I pray for your good instead of revenge because he told me he would be my defense.

Wasted Time

Over the years, I was so immature. My only care was the club scene and hitting the streets. However, as I travel down memory lane I wish those actions I could have changed. To become more serious and independent but I had no cares. Now I wish I could go back to teenage years. Then I would push away my peers. Then plan my life out carefully and when. I got older It has guaranteed that my life be in order. While my friends have a good time I will stay, home planning goals and being persistent to get it done. I would put all my energy into living with a purpose. I would climb the ladder of success I will feel I am too young to rest. Then as my works show progress I would, look back and say I have not wasted time yet.

Melody Toomer

Continue To Act Like You Don't Know Me

When I reach my success and start reaping the benefits. Do not come around saying how are you? You did not believe in my potential now here is the proof. My hard work in the making with my motivation overtaking my life and every day duties I don't operate on proving anything to anyone I want stop until I've done what I set out to do you can give me the cold shoulder. You can be the fool but do not come smiling in my face when my work is done and I have finished this race.

Share Your Thoughts...

Lyrically Spoken

Incarcerated...

Poverty and he is enslaved in his mind! Cannot find a nine to five because he messed up one time. He was confined to a prison defined by the system. Were released and became the victim without a day of relief his pride was eliminated. No longer motivated as because they confiscated his joy. Judged by the majority labeled as a menace to society. He paid his dues followed all the rules vowed to have a brand new life. However, he is deprived. Now, he has to choose because his bills are due and his child is crying with nothing to eat. Then his girl turns and look at him in despair knowing he care's it is time for him to go back out there. Moreover, hustle and grind he had wished he never went to prison that one time.

Now the cycle repeat's he addicted to the fast money lifestyle. Yet living everyday in fear looking over his shoulder hoping he does not run into the bondage approaches with his hand on his hoister. Taking him back to the chain gain thinking they do not want to see us prevail. There only satisfaction is when we fail and when you are caught up and become a second offender. They become ecstatic because you are defenseless and miserable. Cannot find a way of living all because of this crooked system. It is designed to keep the rich, rich and the poor, poor. Everyone knows who was created for. The main objective is to hold you down until your only option is destruction. In the hood somebody is busting, stealing, killing and grinding.

"All because minorities are divided and singled out. I do not care if you are in a suit your still racially profiled."

Words from the Heart

Melody Toomer

Lyrically Spoken

Notes...

Words from the Heart

Melody Toomer

Lyrically Spoken
Share Your Ideas...

Words from the Heart

Melody Toomer

Lyrically Spoken

How Was These Poems Helpful To You?

Words from the Heart

Melody Toomer

Making Changes in Your Life…

Lyrically Spoken
Comments...

Words from the Heart

Melody Toomer

Lyrically Spoken

Words from the Heart

Melody Toomer

Lyrically Spoken

Words from the Heart

www.ingramcontent.com/pod-product-compliance
Lightning Source LLC
Chambersburg PA
CBHW071752040426
42446CB00012B/2524